THE
BUSINESS CASE CHECKLIST

Everything You Need to

Review a Business Case

Avoid Failed Projects

and Turn Technology into ROI

BUSINESS
CASE **PRO**

ABOUT BUSINESS CASE PRO

BUSINESS CASE PRO OFFERS TOOLS AND ADVICE THAT TURN TECHNOLOGY INTO RETURN ON INVESTMENT (ROI). A professional business case is the most powerful tool for both buyers and sellers of technology. For buyers, we advise on writing and reviewing business cases and using them to deliver high-ROI investments. For sellers, we advise on writing business cases that support the sale of technology solutions and value-based pricing.

The principal of Business Case Pro has specialized in writing business cases, selling technology solutions, and pricing IT value for a quarter of a century. He is an Oxford University law graduate and holds several post-graduate financial qualifications, including Chartered Financial Analyst (CFA). Based in the U.S.A., he also works across Europe and Asia.

To protect confidentiality, principal and client names are not publicly disclosed.

Thank you very much for buying The Business Case Checklist.

Any feedback or questions are most welcome at: advice@businesscasepro.com.

Sincerely,

www.businesscasepro.com

TABLE OF CONTENTS

BAD BUSINESS CASES CAN WASTE BILLIONS

6% of CFO's apply formal ROI analysis to most or all of their investments

30% HAVE NO FORMAL APPROACH TO EVALUATING ROI

source: CFO magazine, 2006

ABOUT 30% OF INFORMATION TECHNOLOGY (IT) INVESTMENTS ARE SUCCESSFUL. WITH TOTAL GLOBAL IT SPENDING OVER ONE AND A HALF TRILLION DOLLARS, THIS MEANS WASTING BILLIONS OF DOLLARS A YEAR ON IT INVESTMENTS. BAD BUSINESS CASES, A MAJOR CONTRIBUTOR TO INVESTMENT SHORTFALLS, HAVE THREE KEY AFFLICTIONS:

- **THEY ARE UNDERUSED.** Fewer than half of companies use business cases for all investments. A CFO magazine survey of CFOs in 2006 found that only 6% apply formal return-on-investment (ROI) analysis to most or all of their investments. And 30% have no formal approach to evaluating ROI.

- **THEY ARE UNBELIEVABLE.** PA Management Consultants found that only 40% of survey respondents believed the business cases presented to them. Over optimism about benefits is rampant.

- **THEY ARE POORLY ARGUED.** Business cases are too often couched in technical terminology, lack a unifying argument, and rely on slight evidence and suspect ROI calculations.

WHY USE THE BUSINESS CASE CHECKLIST?

THE BUSINESS CASE CHECKLIST OFFERS REVIEWERS OF IT INVESTMENT THREE MAJOR BENEFITS:

- **FASTER DECISIONS**: much knowledge is condensed, using only essential criteria.

- **A SIMPLE STANDARD INVESTMENT PROCESS**: evaluation criteria are streamlined and consistent.

- **PROFITABLE IT INVESTMENTS**: promotes thorough due diligence and an active approach to investing, which produces high-ROI technology investments.

Checklists are essential for the military, medicine, and aviation. These important tools present information efficiently, reduce errors of omission, create reliable evaluation, and improve quality.

Using this checklist consistently will help your company build professional business cases. A professional business case to justify a proposed investment should include:

- **A BUSINESS AND ECONOMIC RATIONALE FOR THE INVESTMENT**
- **A DEFINITION OF THE INVESTMENT AND ITS FEASIBILITY**
- **A FINANCIAL MODEL QUANTIFYING AND VALUING THE BENEFITS AND COSTS OF THE INVESTMENT**
- **A PLAN FOR DELIVERING BUSINESS AND FINANCIAL VALUE**

A professional business case helps a company determine what it wants to achieve and how, rather than just using the case to obtain funding.

BUY THE BUSINESS CASE BEFORE BUYING TECHNOLOGY

Treat technology as an investment. That way, you are buying the cash flows produced by the technology – the ROI. A business case captures these cash flows. This checklist supports the preparation of a business case for a technology-based investment, including hardware, software, or services. Buyers of technology can use the checklist to review business cases justifying projects and programs. Sellers of technology can use the checklist to improve business cases for sales of their products, services, and solutions.

The checklist is most relevant to technology with substantial benefits, or a top line. This means IT initiatives producing significant new revenue, cost savings, time reductions, or quality improvement. Business cases work best for technology treated as capital expenditure, but they also support technology classified as operating expenditure, such as software-as-a-service.

Where the checklist refers to "the investment," it means the product, service, project, program, or solution proposed in the business case.

WHAT'S BEHIND THE CHECKLIST?

This checklist derives first from the author's quarter of a century experience consulting on IT business cases, solution selling, and value pricing. Second, it is the result of reviewing and distilling several dozen books and other publications about business cases, due diligence, and related areas. See the Selected Bibliography for details.

USING THIS CHECKLIST CONSISTENTLY WILL HELP YOUR COMPANY BUILD PROFESSIONAL BUSINESS CASES

THE UNDERLYING PRINCIPLES

FIVE PRINCIPLES EMERGED TO PROVIDE THE UNDERPINNINGS OF THE CHECKLIST: technology is an investment; value comes from improved process performance; use discounted cash flow analysis to measure value; prepare a business case before any IT capital investment; and the overarching fundamental questions to ask of any IT investment and its business case. Let's consider each of these.

I. TECHNOLOGY IS AN INVESTMENT

The fundamental principle behind The Business Case Checklist is that technology spending is an investment. First, it fits the traditional definition of an investment – commit funds now against future payments, with compensation for time, inflation, and the uncertainty of future cash flows. Second, since shareholders are the legal owners of a firm, technology should – like any corporate expenditure – contribute to shareholder value. Buying technology is asking to put more capital into production processes. Consequently, it requires proper justification, like any investment.

The most robust measure of contribution to shareholder value is discounted cash flow; the value of a business, capital project, or any proposed investment is a function of the amount, timing, and uncertainty of future cash flows. This means that managers should decide about any technology expenditure based on the risk-adjusted present value of its forecasted cash flows.

The threshold for when technology spending moves from an expense to an investment is when the benefits and costs extend beyond one or two years.

II. TECHNOLOGY VALUE COMES FROM IMPROVED PROCESS PERFORMANCE

Technology derives value from improving the inputs, outputs, and outcomes of a process. Every process has some kind of output, whether it is a product, service, analytical report, or other deliverable. Infrastructure investments enable multiple processes.

Investment projects deliver or improve process outputs and outcomes or they make the process itself more efficient and effective. Organizations should value their IT investments based on measurements of changes in the business' performance. The overall approach is illustrated below.

THE FUNDAMENTAL PRINCIPLE BEHIND THE BUSINESS CASE CHECKLIST IS THAT TECHNOLOGY SPENDING IS AN INVESTMENT

1

IDENTIFY THE TARGET PROCESS FOR TECHNOLOGY-BASED INVESTMENT

a. SUPPLIERS → **b. INPUTS** → **c. TARGET PROCESS** → **d. OUTPUTS & OUTCOMES** → **e. CUSTOMERS**

| Organizations, Departments, Individuals, that provide input | Labor, Technology Intellectual Capital Information Financial Capital | Process targeted for investment to improve performance | Outputs are direct, countable and short term Outcomes are harder to count and are medium term | Either External or Internal |

2

OPERATIONAL IMPROVEMENT INPUTS, OUTPUTS, OUTCOMES, AND PROCESS →

MEASURE PERFORMANCE IMPROVEMENTS

3

VALUE OPERATIONAL IMPROVEMENTS AND CONVERT TO FINANCIAL BENEFITS →

VALUE PERFORMANCE IMPROVEMENTS

INPUTS: Resources you need to make something happen. Once measured and priced, they are a cost.

OUTPUTS: Direct result of your objective or project, are countable.
Examples:
Increased unit sales of a product. Higher volumes of transactions processed.

OUTCOMES: Changes that occur over the long term, are harder to count.
Examples:
Improvements in customer experience. More engaged employees.

PROCESS: Steps and activities that transform inputs into outputs and outcomes.

III. USE DISCOUNTED CASH FLOW ANALYSIS TO MEASURE VALUE

Companies buy technology to become better at something and to add to their business plan. The best way to measure increased value from technology is discounted cash flow. You calculate discounted cash flows by identifying the incremental cash flows produced by a project and discounting them to reflect their risk and timing.

Whether or not to invest in a technology project should be decided on the risk-adjusted present value of its forecasted cash flows. Applying discounted cash flow analysis to technology spending simplifies technology buying and selling. A technology may have thousands of features and functions, but only three major ways to create value; it can increase cash flow, accelerate its receipt, or reduce the risks in receiving cash flow.

THE BUSINESS CASE IS A TOOL TO MAKE BETTER CAPITAL EXPENDITURE DECISIONS

IV. USE A BUSINESS CASE WHEN INVESTING IT CAPITAL

The business case is a tool to make better capital expenditure decisions. Typically, capital assets provide long-term benefits to an organization but exhibit a timing delay between the cash outflows and inflows. Writing a business case disciplines technology sellers and buyers to think through an investment proposition and communicate it logically and concisely. A good business case serves as an investment thesis, due diligence tool, and a plan for value delivery. It supports rational, economic decisions rather than stories about features and assertions of value.

V. ASK FUNDAMENTAL QUESTIONS OF ANY IT INVESTMENT AND ITS BUSINESS CASE

When you drill down, fundamental questions must be answered when judging any IT investment and its business case. The checklist focuses on those questions.

Each step in the checklist poses a fundamental question any reviewer should ask of an investment. These questions are:

1. What is the business need?
2. What is the investment that addresses the business need?
3. What technology underlies the investment?
4. What are the benefits of the investment?
5. What are the costs of the investment?
6. What are the major risks?
7. How did we value the investment?
8. Is the investment feasible and a good fit?
9. What alternatives did we consider?
10. How do we execute on the investment?
11. Is this a good business case?
12. Do we invest?

AN INTRODUCTION TO THE CHECKLIST

Before diving into the checklist, here's a brief review of what's involved. We try to answer the usual questions concerning who, when, and how.

WHO SHOULD USE THIS CHECKLIST?

This checklist will benefit:

- Business unit executives funding technology initiatives

- Financial executives and managers reviewing business cases and the supporting financial model

- Technology executives sponsoring IT business cases

- Technology marketers and salespeople wanting to sell more using a believable, compelling business case

- Technology and project managers justifying their technology project or program

WHEN TO USE THIS CHECKLIST?

Whenever you make an IT investment you need a business case. This checklist can help business case reviewers and approvers make faster, better investment decisions. It has most value for larger IT investments (initial expenditure over half a million dollars), but the principles apply to any size of investment.

Here's a short test on whether or not to use a business case: Does the spending behave like a capital investment by producing a multi-period future income stream rather than a single-period expense? If so, then prepare a business case.

WHAT ATTITUDE SHOULD ONE HAVE?

As a reviewer, view yourself as a manager-investor. Take a hard-headed, skeptical attitude, similar to a private equity investor performing due diligence. Look for "investment killers" and holes in the case, especially, excessive optimism on benefits and costs, misstatements, or omissions. As a manager-investor, you should manage IT investments actively, not passively. This means vigorous monitoring of the economic performance of an investment.

TAKE A HARDHEADED, SKEPTICAL ATTITUDE, SIMILAR TO A PRIVATE EQUITY INVESTOR PERFORMING DUE DILIGENCE

WHAT IS THE ROLE IN THE INVESTMENT PROCESS?

This checklist fits into an overall IT investment process as follows:

- As a tool to review individual business cases as they come forward

- Guidelines to assist the judgment of experienced executives, rather than a rigid set of rules

- As a test to screen individual investments before inclusion in any IT portfolio reviews

- To serve as a foundation to design and build a repeatable IT investment process

EACH STEP IN THE CHECKLIST FOCUSES ON A FUNDAMENTAL QUESTION THAT ANY REVIEWER SHOULD ASK OF AN INVESTMENT

HOW IS THE CHECKLIST COMPLETED?

Each step in the checklist focuses on a fundamental question that any reviewer should ask of an investment.

The checklist has 10 questions, or steps, that score an investment. Step 11 grades the business case and Step 12 requires a decision: Do we invest?

WHAT IS AN INVESTMENT QUALITY SCORE?

We recommend scoring how well each step is covered on the following scale:

Section Score	Quality of Coverage
5	Excellent
4	Good
3	Adequate
2	Poor
1	Missing

There is no need to score each sub-step within a section. If you do, you should average them for the section.

WHAT IS A BUSINESS CASE QUALITY GRADE?

The business case grade provides a compact summary of the overall quality of a business case.

Quality Grade	Case Quality
A	Excellent clarity, accuracy, logic, and financial model
B	Good coverage
C	Adequate coverage
D	Poor coverage
E	Missing coverage

HOW TO MAKE AN INVESTMENT DECISION?

The final step in the checklist, Step 12, asks you to add up the score for each step. It allows collection and comparison of business case scores. The total score generates a recommended investment action: full investment, partial investment, resubmit, or reject.

Use the overall investment score and business case grade to inform your decision, not to make it. Remember that any investment decision requires judgment. The investment score is a rating of the strength of the underlying investment and the business case grade assesses the quality of the case. A high score and good grade means that you have a strong investment wrapped in a good case. Combined with an active investment approach, investing is likely to deliver the forecast returns.

USE THE OVERALL INVESTMENT SCORE AND BUSINESS CASE GRADE TO INFORM YOUR DECISION, NOT TO MAKE IT

THE CHECKLIST

STEP 1 : THE BUSINESS NEED

IS THE BUSINESS NEED CLEAR AND UNDERSTOOD?
SEEK EVIDENCE OF:

- A true problem – a difference between actual and desired performance

- A precise problem statement including what, where, and when

- A root-cause analysis-a search for the most basic cause of a problem (see best practices for guidance)

IS THE BUSINESS NEED ACUTE? SEEK EVIDENCE OF:

- A discussion of who is affected by the problem and by how much

- Whether this is a painkiller and addresses a need, or a vitamin and addresses a want.

- Unacceptable baseline performance

WHAT IS THE COMPLICATION? A COMPLICATION IS A CONDITION
THAT MAKES THE STATUS QUO UNBEARABLE.

- Is the complication internal? Examples include:

  - Rapid revenue loss

  - Unacceptable cost or cash burn

  - Risk overload

- Is the complication external? Examples include:

  - Industry contraction

  - Aggressive competitors

WHY SOLVE THIS PROBLEM NOW?

- Is this problem unsustainable?

- Why do you need the money now

SECTION SCORE _____

STEP 2 : THE INVESTMENT

WHAT IS THE SCOPE AND IMPACT OF THE INVESTMENT?
- Can the impact be measured? What needs to change and how can a change be detected?

- Which processes are affected? What is the improvement?

- How does the impact translate to benefits?

WHAT IS THE INVESTMENT PROFILE?
- What is the net present value ("NPV") of the investment?

- What is the internal rate of return ("IRR") of the investment?

- When will the investment pay back?

- What is the useful economic life of the investment?

- Will the investment have any value at the end of its written down or economic life?

HOW MUCH MONEY IS NEEDED?
- Are all inputs (resources) identified and quantified?

- Are all inputs priced and sources documented?

- Are full lifecycle costs captured?

SECTION SCORE _____

STEP 3 : THE TECHNOLOGY

WHAT CHANGE IN PERFORMANCE DOES THIS TECHNOLOGY OFFER?

WHAT TECHNOLOGY ARE WE BUYING? IS THERE A CONCISE, BUSINESS-ORIENTED SUMMARY?
- How mature is the technology?

- How robust is the vendor?

- Do we understand the architectural components of the technology?

- If there are off-the-shelf or open-source components, what is the licensing model? How do we protect ourselves against vendor acquisition or reorganization?

- Is this a solution or a collection of point products? If a solution, is it a whole solution and are there any functional or technical gaps?

- Do we have any security or privacy concerns?

- Is the system global?

WHAT DOES THE TECHNOLOGY DO? LOOK FOR:
- An explanation of the technology's key features and functions, why and how they solve the business problem, and how they translate into benefits

- Evidence of a demonstration, showing that it works

- Identification of the key users of the technology and a description of how they would use it?

DOES THIS TECHNOLOGY HAVE ANY MEASURABLE TECHNICAL DIFFERENCES AGAINST OTHER PRODUCTS OR SOLUTIONS
- Have any such differences been documented?

- Who are its competitors?

- Are there any complementary technologies?

ARE WE READY TO IMPLEMENT THE TECHNOLOGY?
- Does it require significant process and culture changes?

- Will it ride on existing infrastructure and networks?

- Do we have appropriate and up-to-date software versions?

SECTION SCORE _____

STEP 4 : THE BENEFITS

WHAT OPERATING IMPROVEMENTS WILL THE TECHNOLOGY PRODUCE?
- When will they occur?

- Are they quantifiable and how do we measure them?

- Who is responsible for measuring them?

WHERE DO THE BENEFITS COME FROM?
- What are they; when will they occur; where will they occur; and for whom are they?

- Are they quantifiable and how do we measure them?

- How are they derived?

- What is the value of the benefits?

- How are benefits valued?

ARE WE ONLY COUNTING INCREMENTAL BENEFITS COMPARED TO THE NEXT-BEST ALTERNATIVE?

ARE THE BENEFITS COMPLETE, ACCURATE, AND REALISTIC?

SECTION SCORE _____

STEP 5 : THE COSTS

ARE ALL ESTIMATED RESOURCES AND EFFORTS (INPUTS) CAPTURED? INCLUDING:

- People

- Technology

- Capital

- Fixed and variable costs: including establishing their level and forecasting future behavior

WHAT ARE THE SOURCES OF RESOURCE ESTIMATES? APPROACHES INCLUDE

- Engineering-bottom up from the technology

- Analogies with similar previous systems

- Parameter-based

ARE COSTS ACROSS THE FULL LIFECYCLE CAPTURED? INCLUDING:

- Acquisition and development

- Integration and transition

- Operation

- Retirement

HAVE APPROPRIATE CALCULATIONS BEEN COMPLETED? INCLUDING:

- Any added costs the investment will create

- Any scale effects that reduce long-run costs

- Pricing of inputs at opportunity cost or market prices

WHAT ARE THE SOFTWARE COSTS?

- If buying an off-the-shelf application, consider:

    - Licensing costs

    - Maintenance costs

    - Whether any components are provided by partners

    - Whether any components are open source

- If internally developed, consider:

    - The rationale for building in-house: will it provide a competitive advantage in a differentiating process?

    - How the estimate was prepared

- If software-as-a-service, consider:

    - Use for a non-differentiating, commodity process

    - Security and privacy

    - Fixed, periodic (monthly), or per-event or transaction charging

SECTION SCORE _____

STEP 6 : THE RISKS

HAVE THE MAJOR RISKS BY CATEGORY BEEN IDENTIFIED AND DEFINED? INCLUDING:

- Economic: particularly, any excessive benefit, cost, and timing optimism

- Financial: funding availability and affordability

- Technical: evidence that the technology works

- Operational: particularly, the amount of change required and the company's track record of delivering projects of similar scope and complexity

WHAT ARE THE RISKS OF DOING NOTHING?

ARE THE MAJOR RISKS ASSESSED, ADJUSTED, AND ADDRESSED BY A MITIGATION PLAN?

- What is the worst case and is there a plan to mitigate this risk?

- Are they quantifiable and how do we measure them?

- Are the benefits worth the risk?

- Are risks shared where possible?

HAS THERE BEEN A RISK ASSESSMENT USING SENSITIVITY AND SCENARIO ANALYSIS?

ARE WE TAKING A SMALL STEPS APPROACH? HAVE THE FOLLOWING BEEN CONSIDERED?

- Pilots or prototypes to test whether the proposed option works

- Modules: discrete parts of the project that deliver value

- Phased investment and implementation

- Multiple exit points from the investment

SECTION SCORE _____

STEP 7 : THE VALUATION

HAVE THE COSTS AND BENEFITS OF THE INVEST-MENT PROJECT BEEN TRANSLATED INTO CASH FLOWS?

WHAT ARE THE RISKS OF DOING NOTHING?

ARE THE CASH FLOWS INCREMENTAL? I.E.,
- Is there a difference in cash flows for your company with and without the investment project.

- Only future costs and benefits are relevant.

WHAT ARE THE ASSUMPTIONS ON CASH FLOW TIMING? A COMMON ASSUMPTION IS THAT CASH FLOWS OCCUR AT THE END OF EACH QUARTER OR YEAR.

WHAT RATE IS USED TO CALCULATE THE PRESENT VALUES OF CASH FLOWS?
- Is it the corporate hurdle rate?

- How does the risk of this investment compare to other corporate investments-the same, higher, or lower?

- Is the discount rate appropriate to the risk of the investment cash flows?

IS TAX TREATED CONSISTENTLY? EITHER DISCOUNT PRE-TAX CASH FLOWS WITH A PRE-TAX COST OF CAPITAL OR POST-TAX CASH FLOWS WITH A POST-TAX COST OF CAPITAL.

WHAT ABOUT TERMINAL VALUES? IS THERE AN ASSUMPTION OF THE ASSET HAVING VALUE AT THE END OF THE DISCOUNTING PERIOD?

SECTION SCORE _____

STEP 8 : FEASIBILITY & FIT

ECONOMIC FEASIBILITY: WILL THE INVESTMENT MAKE MONEY?

- Does the investment have a positive net present value ("NPV")? How much?

- What are the expected, optimistic, and pessimistic NPVs?

- Is the internal rate of return ("IRR") sufficiently high?

FINANCIAL: CAN WE AFFORD THE INVESTMENT?

- Can we obtain the budget?

- Does it fit our budget cycle?

- Who will pay for the project? Have they agreed to do so, and how?

- What is the plan for funding cash deficits caused by benefit-cost timing mismatches?

ASSET FEASIBILITY: WILL IT WORK?

- If it works, will it solve the problem? In full, or partially?

- Is it reliable and secure?

- Will it scale?

OPERATIONAL: CAN WE DO IT? LOOK FOR:

- An assessment of the capability (skills and expertise needed) and capacity (number of people required over the lifetime of the project) to execute the investment

- A project management structure identifying key roles and responsibilities

- A realistic implementation plan with a clear scope and including all major activities

- Defined deliverables: is success in terms of outputs and outcomes well defined?

- A risk management plan: have we identified the major risks and do we have a successful track record in managing them?

- Evidence of senior management sponsorship

IS THE INVESTMENT A GOOD STRATEGIC FIT? LOOK FOR:

- Linking of the investment to corporate, business unit, and technology strategies

- An explanation of company goals addressed by the investment

- An outline of how the investment contributes to a core business capability

- How the investment yields a competitive advantage

DOES THE INVESTMENT FIT OUR ENTERPRISE ARCHITECTURE?:

- Are there any infrastructure effects or any modifications required?

DOES THE INVESTMENT FIT OUR IT PORTFOLIO?

- Does it overlap with any existing investments?

- Will the technology work with our existing systems? Easily, or with difficulty?

SECTION SCORE _____

STEP 9 : ALTERNATIVES

WHAT IS THE NEXT-BEST ALTERNATIVE TO THE PROPOSED INVESTMENT? THE MOST LIKELY CANDIDATES ARE:
- Refreshed status quo with costs and benefits projected into the future

- A competing third-party solution

HAVE WE CALCULATED THE NPV OF THE NEXT-BEST ALTERNATIVE?

IN ADDITION TO THE NEXT-BEST ALTERNATIVE, DID WE REVIEW A MINIMUM SET OF ALTERNATIVES?
- Unchanged status quo

- Best: strong solution, but costly with large payoffs

- Cheap: cheaper solution, but less effective

DID WE DO A MARKET SOUNDING AND REVIEW ALL FEASIBLE ALTERNATIVES? INCLUDING:
- Taking action, but using a non-capital alternative such as:

    - Contracting out

    - Divesting or outsourcing the problem

- Improving the asset

- Replacing the asset by buying or building a new one

- Full-potential state: defined by benchmarking to best practices and performance levels

- An innovative alternative based on an alternative technology or concept

SECTION SCORE _____

STEP 10 : INVESTMENT EXECUTION

IS THERE A SOLID IMPLEMENTATION PLAN? LOOK FOR:
- A sharply defined project scope

- Fixed milestones: is the release of new funds contingent on achieving milestones?

- Phased investment: with each chunk having independent value

- A recognition of constraints such as timescales and resources

- A realistic, affordable cost estimate

- A careful analysis of risks and barriers

- A few, vital indicators of success

WHAT IS THE PLAN FOR REALIZING BENEFITS? LOOK FOR:
- Judgment on how much change the investment requires

- Mechanisms to validate the benefits model in stages

- Pre-set thresholds for intervention, including:

    - Maximum investment cost variance (a cost ceiling)

    - Minimum expected benefit achieved (a benefit floor)

WHAT ABOUT COMMITMENTS AND CONTRACTS?
- Is there a delivery contract that covers who does what and how benefits, costs, and risks are allocated?

- Is the contract well designed and likely to deliver the specified outputs/outcomes on time, within budget, and to provide value for money?

SECTION SCORE _____

STEP 11 : BUSINESS CASE QUALITY (GRADE A TO E, NOT SCORE)

ARE ALL THE CRITICAL COMPONENTS OF A QUALITY BUSINESS CASE PRESENT? LOOK FOR:
- Clarity

- Accuracy

- Logic

- A sound financial model

CLARITY – LOOK FOR A CLEAR AND CONCISE PRESENTATION:
- Is information boiled down to encourage clear thinking and crisp communication?

- Does the case have an effective summary?

    - Is there an attention-worthy headline?

    - Is there a focus on what's new?

    - Is the "so what" question handled well?

- Is the conclusion and recommended action precise and clear?

ACCURACY – LOOK FOR:
- Evidence:

    - Will the solution solve the problem?

    - What is the evidence for this claim?

    - Have the stakeholders approved and committed to the expected benefits of the project?

    - Are data sources identified and documented? What is their quality and diversity?

    - Are distinctions between facts, vendor opinions, and judgments by the business case writer clear?

- Robust assumptions:

    - Are assumptions articulated?

    - Are load-bearing (critical) assumptions highlighted?

    - What is the source of the assumptions? Was there a business discovery to define them? Are the sources credible?

    - Are the assumptions realistic and expressed as a range?

LOGIC:
- Is the case concise and logically argued? Look for logical linkage among:

    - The statement of the problem or need addressed

    - An explanation of the causes of the problem

    - A complication: why the current situation is unsustainable

    - The recommended solution to the problem

    - The benefits of the recommendation

A SOUND FINANCIAL MODEL:
- Is the investment recommendation based on a rigorous and objective NPV assessment? Including:

    - Estimates of incremental cash flows from the project

    - A risk assessment of project cash flows and a determination of the required rate of return (cost of capital)

    - A calculation of the present value of the expected future cash flows

    - A comparison of the cost of the project to what the project is worth: If the project is worth more than it costs (positive NPV), it is worth undertaking.

    - IRR calculation

- A payback calculation showing where and when the investment produces positive cash flows

- A complete financial model, including:

    - All benefits-primarily quantitative, but also qualitative

    - Full costs-including upfront, ongoing, and indirect

BUSINESS CASE GRADE _____

STEP 12 : THE INVESTMENT DECISION

ADD UP THE SCORES FOR EACH STEP IN THE CHECKLIST.

Grade the quality and presentation of the business case.

Determine the total investment score.

Apply the suggested investment decision below.

Note that the maximum investment score is 50.

TOTAL SCORE _____

Investment Score	Business Case Grade	Recommended Investment Action
Greater than or equal to 40	A or B	Full investment
Greater than or equal to 30	A B or C	Partial investment (good parts only) or resubmit in full, after reworking investment and case
Below 30	D or E	Reject

A GUIDE TO BEST PRACTICES

THIS GUIDE PROVIDES COMMENTARY AND BEST PRACTICES
FOR IMPLEMENTING THE BUSINESS CASE CHECKLIST.
THE BEST PRACTICES ARE EVIDENCE-BASED, WHETHER
ACTUAL EXPERIENCE OR DERIVED FROM RESEARCH.

STEP ONE: THE BUSINESS NEED

FIXING A PROBLEM STARTS WITH A PRECISE STATEMENT OF THE BUSINESS NEED.
There are three reasons for this. First, solutions do not exist in a vacuum; their value comes from the value of the problem solved. Second, an opaque or incomplete problem analysis risks never fixing the problem. Third, if key stakeholders do not endorse the business need, a successful investment is unlikely.

The business need section can have a different name – problem, need, or requirement – but each must answer the question: What makes this work and investment necessary?

BEST PRACTICES

1. **ALWAYS START WITH THE QUESTION:** What problem are we solving? Not what product or service are we selling? A problem is not the absence of a solution.

2. **DETERMINE THE DEGREE OF NEED.** Is it mild, chronic, or acute? Acute means the current state is too painful to bear. If it is chronic, then look for a complication that makes the status quo unsustainable.

3. **MEASURE THE CURRENT BASELINE PERFORMANCE** and estimate the impact of not addressing the need.

4. **USE A ROOT CAUSE ANALYSIS TO ADDRESS THE REAL PROBLEM,** not a superficial, pre-packaged version. A root cause is the most basic reasons for an event or effect which, if corrected, will prevent recurrence. Fundamentally, a root cause is nothing more than a series of questions. What happened? When did it happen? Who caused it to happen? And, most importantly, why did it happen? Avoiding a root cause analysis means making assumptions about a problem. Every assumption is a source of risk.

5. **SOLVE ONLY PROBLEMS ACKNOWLEDGED BY SENIOR STAKEHOLDERS.**

6. **CHECK THAT THE INVESTMENT/PROJECT REQUIREMENTS ARE DIRECTLY TRACEABLE TO BUSINESS OBJECTIVES.**

7. **IS THERE A NOT STATEMENT?** For example, NOT investing in this project will result in not achieving objectives (give examples), which means bad things (describe) will happen.

STEP TWO: THE INVESTMENT

PROFILE THE INVESTMENT, INCLUDING THE OPPORTUNITIES, RISKS, AND UNCERTAINTIES.

BEST PRACTICES

8. UNDERSTAND THE SCOPE OF IMPACT:

- Which business units/functions will be impacted?

- Which processes will be affected?

- Explain the cause-and-effect between the investment and its outputs or outcomes.

9. SPECIFY THE INVESTMENT LOGIC, INCLUDING:

- What is put into the investment (resources)?

- What does the investment do (activities and outputs)?

- What changes (outcomes) does the investment hope to achieve?

- What is the cause-and-effect model? What is the desired result? What factors cause the result?

10. TEST ANY RETURN NUMBERS OR CAUSAL CLAIMS MADE BY THE SELLER.

- Ask them to explain the specific linkage between the technology underlying the investment and the results.

11. BEWARE OF OUTLANDISH ROI CLAIMS.
Review the reasonableness of NPV and IRR returns. Consider comparable projects and investments. Consider expected returns from venture capitalists as ceilings for reasonable returns.

REMEMBER THE TIME REQUIRED TO DOUBLE YOUR MONEY AT DIFFERENT IRRS:

- 10% IRR means doubling your money in 7 years

- 20% IRR means doubling your money in 4 years

- 40% IRR means doubling your money in 2 years

- 100% IRR means doubling your money in 1 year

12. CONSIDER ANY PROJECTED ROI (with discounted cash flows) with annual return exceeding 40% as a speculative investment. Check all assumptions, especially whether or not all costs in the maintenance phase are included.

Investment Stage	Expected annual IRR	Expected return in multiples of initial investment
Developing product	70%	Over 10x in 5 years
Revenue customers	50%	Need 5x in 4 years
Expansion	40%	Need 3x in 3 years
Mature business	25%	Need 1.25x in 12 months

STEP THREE: THE TECHNOLOGY

THIS STEP IS A MINI DUE DILIGENCE ON A PROPOSED TECHNOLOGY AND ADDRESSES HOW TECHNOLOGY HELPS A COMPANY BECOME A BETTER BUSINESS. The concept of due diligence comes from securities law, where the due diligence defense requires defendants to prove they exercised reasonable care. Technology managers need to take similar care in understanding what a technology can do for them and what it cannot.

> **TECHNOLOGY MANAGERS NEED TO TAKE SIMILAR CARE IN UNDERSTANDING WHAT A TECHNOLOGY CAN DO FOR THEM AND WHAT IT CANNOT**

BEST PRACTICES

13. **UNDERSTAND EXACTLY WHAT YOU ARE BUYING:**

    • Software applications

    • Data, information, knowledge, best practices

    • Security

    • Communication

    • Infrastructure

    • Technology services

14. **DETERMINE THE MATURITY OF THE TECHNOLOGY. A MODIFIED FRAMEWORK BASED ON THE NASA TECHNOLOGY READINESS FRAMEWORK IS:**

    0. Unproven concept – basic R&D, a paper concept

    1. Proven concept – as a paper study or R&D experiments

    2. Validated concept – experimental proof of concept using physical model tests

    3. Prototype tested – prototype built to assess degree to which application requirements are met and potential benefits and risks demonstrated

    4. Environment tested – tested in simulated or actual environment

    5. System tested – integrated into intended operating system with full interface and functional test but outside intended field environment

    6. System installed – production system installed and tested, but operating for fewer than three years

    7. Field proven – production system field-proven for over three years

15. LOOK FOR SPECIFIC EXAMPLES ON HOW THE TECHNOLOGY WILL BE USED:

- Look for specific use cases illustrating how the technology could or should be employed. Can you clearly identify the potential users?

- Minimize technology evaluations based on subjective persuasion, including manager or vendor opinions or demonstrations in unrealistic environments. Use a pilot project to generate high-quality evidence in a near-production environment.

16. SEEK A CLEAR EXPLANATION OF HOW THE PROPOSED TECHNOLOGY WILL MEET YOUR BUSINESS NEEDS:

- Translate technical features and functions into operational benefits. Technology features are insufficient to understand value; you need to understand how features are used and what benefits accrue from their use.

17. ANALYZE WHETHER OR NOT THE TECHNOLOGY IS DIFFERENTIATING. Think generally and specifically about the technology's relative advantage. As summed up in Levy and Murnane's The New Division of Labor: "Theory of reorganization [of work] is straightforward: choose an organizational goal; allow computers to carry out rules-based tasks; allow people to concentrate on their comparative advantage-expert thinking and complex communication."

18. EXERCISE DILIGENCE ABOUT WHO YOU ARE BUYING TECHNOLOGY FROM. What are their capabilities and experience? If you are planning a long-term relationship, ensure that they are financially stable. Define their licensing model and check whether or not significant functional upgrades are included in the maintenance fee.

19. ENSURE THAT THE PRODUCT OR SOLUTION ARCHITECTURE IS EXPLICITLY DOCUMENTED:

- Are all the main elements and standards included?

- Is this a custom build? What commercially available off-the-shelf technology is used?

- Are there any open-source components?

20. IDENTIFY AND ASSESS TECHNICAL RISK. Technical risk means cost and schedule uncertainty. The best means of sharing technical risk is to share the cost risk.

21. LOOK FOR FULL SOLUTIONS THAT CAPTURE THE FULL PROBLEM VALUE. TRY TO AVOID LEAVING VALUE GAPS.

THE BEST MEANS OF SHARING TECHNICAL RISK IS TO SHARE THE COST RISK

STEP FOUR: THE BENEFITS

BENEFITS ARE THE RETURN FROM AN INVESTMENT.
They are the equivalent of revenue projections in a business plan. They are measurable performance improvements which, once they have a financial value, become bankable benefits.

BEST PRACTICES

22. BUILD A COMPLETE AND REALISTIC BENEFITS MODEL:

- Define the source and type of benefit:

    - Benefits come from doing or deferring something new or improving, reducing, or divesting something existing.

    - Benefits save money, make money, or improve customer relationships.

    - Are the benefits primarily business or technical or a mixture?

    - Benefits are often industry-specific. For example, benefits of fast response time vary across industries because of differences in the time value of information.

- For each benefit, determine the size, timing, and likelihood of achievement:

    - Size: Quantify in a forecast of net cash flows. Benefit/sales projections need number of output units and a value or price per unit.

    - Timing: Forecast time schedule of cash flows.

    - Likelihood of achievement: Compute the probability of various outcomes, such as optimistic, expected, and pessimistic.

23. REVIEW THE REALISM OF THE BENEFITS:

- Do you believe the numerical forecast of the benefits you are buying?

- Are the assumptions realistic, logical, attainable, and either consistent with industry norms or with deviations that can be explained.

- Are valuation methods clearly described and reasonable?

BENEFITS ARE THE EQUIVALENT OF REVENUE PROJECTIONS IN A BUSINESS PLAN

24. ESTABLISH LINKAGES BETWEEN IMPACTS TO OUTCOMES/OUTPUTS AND BENEFITS:

- Return comes from an impact, which produces benefits.

- Linkages must be defined so managers know how and when they will get the benefits.

- Linkages to supporting business initiatives must be clarified, communicated, and sold.

25. PREPARE A BENEFITS MANAGEMENT PLAN COVERING:

- A profile of outputs and outcomes and how they translate into benefits.

- Defined benefit metrics.

- Clear signposts as to whether or not benefit assumptions are working.

- One senior stakeholder who is accountable for realizing the benefits.

- An active approach to realizing benefits– benefits do not just happen.

- Handling of variances when benefits happen differently from plan.

- Awareness that benefits realization requires more business and organizational understanding than the traditional project management focus on outputs or deliverables.

26. ASSUME BENEFITS ARE OPTIMISTIC. Counter this by using range or scenario estimates for benefits. Scenarios for the expected case, best case, and worst case are usually sufficient.

DO YOU BELIEVE THE NUMERICAL FORECAST OF THE BENEFITS YOU ARE BUYING

STEP FIVE: COSTS

EARNING A RETURN HAS A PRICE. THIS PRICE HAS THREE COMPONENTS. First, it requires cash (costs) to begin and operate the investment. Second, any investment requires capital, which demands a return. Third, any uncertain activity creates risk, which deserves a price and inclusion in the cost of capital calculation.

BEST PRACTICES

27. CALCULATE COSTS CORRECTLY:

- Use incremental costs: the difference between the total costs the firm would incur if it did not make the investment and the total cost if it does.

- Measure opportunity costs: the extent to which an opportunity to use resources for some other purpose has been given up-and not purely financial costs.

- Ignore sunk costs: what must be given up today and the future is relevant; what has already been given up (sunk costs) is irrelevant.

- Ignore overheads: costs either do or do not increase as a result of the investment. Only charge incremental costs to an investment decision.

28. CAPTURE THE FULL LIFE-CYCLE COSTS OF A SYSTEM INCLUDING THE BUILD, IMPLEMENT, OPERATE, AND RETIRE STAGES. Think beyond how much different technologies cost now, but rather how much they will ultimately cost.

29. CAPTURE ALL COST ELEMENTS:

- Software
    - Purchase price and license fees
    - Maintenance and upgrade charges

- Hardware
    - Purchase price
    - Maintenance and upgrade charges

- Support costs, both internal and external
    - Installation and set up
    - Maintenance
    - Troubleshooting
    - Support tools

RETURN HAS A PRICE COSTS CAPITAL AND RISK

- Staff costs
  - Project management
  - Engineering/development
  - System administration
  - Procurement
  - Training

30. UNDERSTAND THE ESTIMATION TECHNIQUE USED FOR COSTS.

Albert Lederer and Jayesh Prasad (reported in McConnell) found that informal comparison of a new project with a similar past project, based solely on personal memory, was used by 83% of estimators. This technique was not found to correlate with accurate estimates. On a positive note, researchers found that significant accuracy differences between intuitive expert judgment (usually inaccurate) and "structured expert judgment" can produce estimates that are about as accurate as model-based estimates (Jorgensen 2002, reported in McConnell).

31. EXERCISE EXTREME SKEPTICISM ON ALL COST ESTIMATES:

- Verify that costs appear consistent with the work effort and plan and technical complexity?

- Treat unrealistically low cost estimates as undesirable as unreasonably high costs.

- Watch for schedule uncertainty; it inevitably gives rise to cost uncertainty.

- Check for unrealistic targets and unachievable commitments. In a study of 300 software projects, Michael van Genuchten reported that developer estimates tended to contain an optimism factor of 20% to 30%.

- Take a long and broad view of all costs and consider delayed consequences.

32. ASK CRITICAL QUESTIONS FOR INDIVIDUAL COST ITEMS (MODIFIED FROM MCCONNELL):

- What is it that we are estimating for?

- Does the estimate include all the kinds of work needed to complete the task?

- Does the estimate include all the functional areas needed to complete the task?

- Is the estimate broken down into enough detail to expose hidden work?

WATCH FOR SCHEDULE UNCERTAINTY IT INEVITABLY GIVES RISE TO COST UNCERTAINTY

BE MANIC DEPRESSIVE ABOUT COST ESTIMATES

- Did you look at documented facts from past work rather than estimating purely from memory?

- Is the estimate approved by the person who will actually do the work?

- Is the productivity assumed in the estimate similar to what has been achieved on similar assignments?

- Does the estimate include an expected case, bad case, and worse case?

- Have the assumptions in the estimate been documented?

- Has the situation changed since the estimate was prepared?

33. **BE MANIC DEPRESSIVE ABOUT COST ESTIMATES.** Use range or scenario estimates for total costs. Given the research on the accuracy of cost estimation, use expected case, bad case, and worse case cost paths.

34. **DISTINGUISH BETWEEN FIXED AND VARIABLE COSTS:**

  - Fixed costs are expenses unaffected by changes in a firm's output.

  - Variable (or incremental) costs vary with changes in output, though not necessarily in direct proportion to output.

35. **PROVIDE CLEAR EVIDENCE OF HOW COST INFORMATION WAS OBTAINED AND ESTIMATED.**

36. **CHECK MARKET PRICES.** When inputs have market prices, the best measure of cost is usually that price. If buying technology from a third party, compare the quoted price to the value created. If developing software in-house, try to put a market price on each component or development module.

37. **FOCUS ON INPUTS THAT, IF MISESTIMATED, WILL HAVE A MATERIAL IMPACT ON COSTS.** For example, in software development, typically, the cost of labor dominates.

STEP SIX: THE RISKS

RISK IS FUTURE UNCERTAINTY (EMANUEL DERMAN).
Initiatives are not equal when it comes to the likelihood of delivering business value or the probability of meeting cost and schedule targets. These factors are the root cause of risk.

Investors cannot know what the return on investment ("ROI") of an investment will be ahead of time; they only know a projected one. This creates risks in achieving the projected ROI at the time of the investment.

A robust, clear business case minimizes risk, identifies potential deal killers, and greatly increase the odds of successful outcomes and high investment returns.

BEST PRACTICES

38. BUILD A RISK PLAN DOCUMENTING THINKING ON MAJOR RISKS AND HOW THEY WILL BE HANDLED. CHIEF RISKS INCLUDE:

- Delivery risk: the risk of not delivering the required capabilities. Signs of delivery risk include:

    - Incomplete or unfeasible program and project plans

    - Ambiguous scope and deliverables

    - Unproven technology

    - A large project relative to team size and capabilities

    - Casual involvement of senior business people

    - Vague availability commitments from key staff

    - Excessive vendor reliance

- Benefits risk: the risk of not achieving the expected benefits. Signs of benefits risk include:

    - Missing, incomplete, or vague measures of outputs and outcomes

    - No benefits monitoring process

    - No sensitivity analysis of outcomes to changes in assumptions

    - Significant organizational change required

39. TAKE SMALL STEPS TO REDUCE RISKS:

- Use pilots (a small-scale initial data collection effort) and prototypes.

- Stage investments.

- Create multiple, clear exit points and watch potential break up values.

- Share risks.

Staged investment mean that at the end of each phase, you decide whether or not to exercise the option to invest in the next phase. This means that you can drop or alter concepts if they do not work.

Research by Capers Jones shows that the larger the project, the less chance the project has of completing on time and the greater the chance it has of failing outright.

The small steps approach uses information to reduce risk.

AVOID DISTRACTIONS LIKE MONTE CARLO SIMULATION

40. FOCUS ON IDENTIFYING THE LOAD-BEARING ASSUMPTIONS:

- "An assumption is load bearing if its failure would require significant changes in the organization's plans"-Assumption-Based Planning by John Dewar. The risk created by a load-bearing assumption is a combination of how much load the assumption carries (its importance to achieving the case) and how likely it is to fail within the time horizon of the case.

41. DO NOT GO OVERBOARD ON RISK MANAGEMENT:

- Try to combine an attitude of maximizing return while reducing risk. The principle is to reduce the probability of bad events through active management.

- Avoid distractions like Monte Carlo simulation. A source of pleasure for the academically minded, it has little practical value for an IT project, with minimal probability data and the ability to influence outcomes.

- The net present value (NPV) of an investment project is the present value of the expected future cash flows, discounted at the cost of capital, net of the amount of any initial investment.

STEP SEVEN: VALUATION

VALUE EXPRESSES THE WORTH OF SOMETHING. Expressing benefits and costs in financial terms is the core of any business case. Business case valuation has three aspects. First, you need to value the outputs and outcomes produced by the investment. Second, you need to put a price on all the resources invested. Third, offsetting the benefits against costs gives you the net projected cash flows from the investment. These cash flows need adjustment for risk and timing. For risk, the probability of earning a cash flow varies by investment. For time, future cash has less value than cash received today.

In buying an investment, one is making a lump sum payment for a future income stream. The investment will make money if the present value of the income stream is more than the current price. So, to assess value, one has to estimate that income stream, take its present value, and compare it to the price to assess its cheapness.

As for any investment, risk-adjusted ROI is the only measurement that matters.

BEST PRACTICES

42. EVALUATE INVESTMENT PROJECTS IN TERMS OF THE CASH THEY ARE EXPECTED TO GENERATE. Because projects differ in the timing and risk of their cash flows, it is necessary to discount the returns to present value to compare them meaningfully.

43. USE BOTH FORMS OF DISCOUNTED CASH FLOW ANALYSIS TO EVALUATE AN INVESTMENT:

- The net present value (NPV) of an investment project is the present value of the expected future cash flows, discounted at the cost of capital, net of the amount of any initial investment.

- The internal rate of return (IRR) is the value of the discount rate that yields an NPV of zero for an investment project. The IRR can be understood as the effective rate of interest earned on the investment, irrespective of the cost of capital. It is an "internal" rate determined only by the project's own cash flows − unlike the cost of capital, which is the competitive rate of return determined by the capital markets.

44. BUILD A COMPLETE FINANCIAL MODEL FOR THE INVESTMENT:

- Develop cash flow projections for the life of the new or improved technology asset.

- Allocate the periodic benefits and costs into time buckets whether monthly, quarterly, or annually.

- Forecast capital and operating expenses for the life of the asset.

- Quantify and adjust for risk through the weighted average cost of capital, which reflects the company's cost of debt and equity and the relative amount of each financing source employed.

- Discount cash flows and calculate the NPV.

45. EXCLUDE ITEMS THAT DO NOT GIVE RISE TO CASH EXPENDITURE, SUCH AS DEPRECIATION AND AMORTIZATION.

46. ACCOUNT FOR ANY TERMINAL OR RESIDUAL VALUE. Residual value is the present value of expected net cash flows during the years of economic life outside the reference period. The reference period is the number of years for which forecasts are provided in the cost benefit analysis.

STEP EIGHT: FEASIBILITY & FIT

THIS STEP ANSWERS THE QUESTION: DOES THIS INVESTMENT MAKE SENSE FOR US? Sense consists of feasibility and fit. Feasibility tests whether the investment is possible and practical; fit determines whether the investment matches your goals and environment.

BEST PRACTICES

47. CONSIDER EVERY DIMENSION OF FEASIBILITY:

- Will the investment make money? This is economic feasibility; a corporate investor requires a rate of return at least as great as the percentage return that can be earned in comparable investment opportunities.

- Will it work? This is technical feasibility; is the product/solution feasible at the price, quality, schedule, and resource level specified in the business case?

- Can we do it? This is operational feasibility; do we have the capability, experience, will, and senior-stakeholder support to deliver this investment?

- Can we afford it? This is financial feasibility; do we have the budget and funds to finance starting, building, and operating this investment.

48. CONSIDER EVERY DIMENSION OF FIT:

- Does the investment support our strategy? All IT-enabled investments should contribute to at least one of a company's strategic objectives. There should be an explicit link between the expected results of an IT investment and business strategy.

- Is it consistent with our enterprise architecture? "Enterprise architecture refers to the way relationships among components of an organization, including processes, people, and technology, work together to create services and/or products" (ValIT).

CAN WE DO IT?

This is operational feasibility; do we have the capability, experience, will, and senior-stakeholder support to deliver this investment?

STEP NINE: ALTERNATIVES

WITHOUT ALTERNATIVES, THERE IS NO DECISION. ALTERNATIVES PROVIDE THE RAW MATERIAL FOR AN INVESTMENT DECISION. Due diligence requires answering the question: why is this the best alternative?

BEST PRACTICES

49. **THINK THOROUGHLY ABOUT ALTERNATIVES.** Michael Scriven provides a useful framework and places alternatives under four broad categories:

    • The "Rolls Royce"– state of the art or best practice performance

    • The 'Shoestring"– a creative low-budget option

    • "A Little More"– an option that has slightly more resources allocated to it

    • "A Little Less"– a slightly more streamlined or economical version of the proposed solution

50. **CONSIDER THE COST OF INACTION AND THE PRICE OF MARKET DELAY.**

51. **RESIST THE EASY OPTIONS, SUCH AS:**
    - Status quo
    - First possible solution
    - Packaged alternatives presented by vested interests

52. **ALWAYS ASK:**

    • Are the claimed constraints real?

    • Who is being paid for what and who gains most from a particular alternative?

    • What is the consensus view and why?

WITHOUT ALTERNATIVES THERE IS NO DECISION

STEP TEN: INVESTMENT EXECUTION

A BUSINESS CASE IS A FORECAST OR PROJECTION BUT, WITHOUT EXECUTION, IT IS JUST AN OPTION ON POTENTIAL RETURNS.

BEST PRACTICES

LOOK FOR COMMITMENTS AND CONTRACTS

53. DEVELOP THE VITAL FEW MEASURES BASED ON TRACKING:

- Economy: relationship between resources and inputs – the cost of inputs

- Efficiency: relationship between inputs and outputs – how well the investment performs with the given inputs

- Effectiveness: relationship between outputs and outcomes – how it contributes to business and strategic goals

54. USE THE BUSINESS CASE TO EXECUTE. As Boehm points out: "use the project's business case analysis as the basis of accumulating projected business value, rather than the current measure of success in terms of task-achievement based value."

55. USE ASSUMPTION-BASED PLANNING.

- An assumption is "a judgment or evaluation about some characteristic of the future that underlies the plans of an organization" (RAND).

- Look for the "load-bearing assumptions" underlying the business case. These are assumptions that would require major changes in your plan or case if they failed. You need to think through what, why, and how these assumptions might fail.

- Define indicators (signposts) to show when an assumption is in trouble. Check these signposts frequently, usually monthly, depending on the length of the project.

- Review business cases for words like "will" and "must;" assumptions often lurk beneath them.

56. LOOK FOR COMMITMENTS AND CONTRACTS. Different contracting approaches are appropriate depending on the context:

- Contract for outcomes when both parties want to partner and influence long-term outcomes. Both requirements and organizations must be stable.

- Contract for outputs when requirements are stable, the process is clear, and the vendor can influence or control the output.

- Contracting for inputs applies when requirements are unstable or the vendor has no influence on outputs/outcomes, or the buyer simply does not want a deeper relationship with the vendor.

57. DO NOT FORCE PREMATURE COMMITMENTS. Early on in projects, not enough work has been done to reduce uncertainty – the "Cone of Uncertainty" in the software estimation literature.

58. PREPARE A SOLID, SIMPLE PROJECT PLAN (OR SUMMARY) SHOWING THE FUNDAMENTAL TASKS, MAJOR COSTS, AND CRITICAL SCHEDULE COMPONENTS. A 1,000-step, multi-colored Gantt chart is not the best start.

59. STAGE INVESTMENTS:

- Only scale up commitments as risks decrease. Use phased investment structures with defined milestones.

- Staged investment has several advantages:

  - It motivates project managers to work on delivering returns.

  - It creates options to abandon the project or revalue the project and commit further capital at each funding stage.

  - It ensures that the NPV of the investment remains positive at each refunding.

60. CARRY OUT BEFORE-AND-AFTER STUDIES: COMPARES COSTS AND OUTCOMES BEFORE AND AFTER THE INTERVENTION. Looking to answer the fundamental question: Did the projected business case show up in the income statement as increased revenue or lower costs? How, where, and when?

USE THE BUSINESS CASE TO EXECUTE

STEP ELEVEN:
BUSINESS CASE QUALITY

TO MAKE THE BEST INVESTMENT DECISION, A REVIEWER MUST ASSESS BOTH THE QUALITY OF THE CASE AND THE VALUE OF THE INVESTMENT RECOMMENDATION. This step focuses on assessing whether or not a business case is written to a professional standard.

CLARITY

Clarity is a gateway standard. If a business case is unclear, then it is difficult to determine whether an investment is good or bad. Reviewers find it difficult to focus exclusively on the merits of an investment without considering the quality of the writing and presentation used to express those merits. As in law, where bad briefs lose good cases; bad business cases sacrifice good investments. A good business case greatly improves your chances of making and executing a good investment.

BEST PRACTICE

ASK EACH BUSINESS CASE WRITER TO INCLUDE THE SHORTEST, SHARPEST SUMMARY POSSIBLE

61. **ASK EACH BUSINESS CASE WRITER TO INCLUDE THE SHORTEST, SHARPEST SUMMARY POSSIBLE, IDEALLY TWO PAGES AND NO MORE THAN THREE.** Reviewers of business cases are in the business of making decisions, not processing reams of undigestable information.

62. **AS FOR ALL WRITING, ENCOURAGE BUSINESS CASE WRITERS TO CONVEY THE MAXIMUM AMOUNT OF INFORMATION WITH THE FEWEST WORDS.** Long-winded writing wastes expensive executive time and is, as Richard Lanham points out, a form of self-deception: "thinking more has been thought and said, and paid for, than in fact has been."

ACCURACY

Accuracy has several attributes:

• Evidence: Avoid unsubstantiated statements. What counts is what works.

• Precision: Are sufficient details provided to deal with the complexities of the issue?

• Complete: Are all factors included? Are alternatives considered?

63. ASSESS THE QUALITY OF EVIDENCE OFFERED BY THE TECHNOLOGY VENDOR, IN ASCENDING ORDER OF DESIRABILITY:
- Description of the products and services offered
- Reference customers
- Customer testimonials
- Actual results documented
- Results documented by an independent evaluator

LOGIC

"Logic is concerned with the soundness of the claims we make...with the sort of case we present in defense of our claims" (Stephen Toulmin).

A logical business case should show the relationship between the problem, the solution components, and the improved situation.

BEST PRACTICES

64. ENSURE THAT THE CORE THEORY OF THE CASE OR "THE BIG IDEA" IS CLEAR. If the case is unsound on its strongest arguments, it will not work with its weaker arguments.

65. ASK WHETHER THE REASONING AND EVIDENCE COMPEL THE CONCLUSION: make this investment and supply the capital requested.

SOUND MODEL

Models are a good way to explore the possible consequences of decisions and plans before taking any action. Their purpose is to aid rational thinking by providing an accurate picture of the financial strength of a proposed investment. They do not set out to forecast the future with complete accuracy.

Every technology business case has a financial model of the projected ROI. A financial model quantifies the relationship between the benefits, costs, risks, and assumptions for an investment project.

Given the amount of work required, a financial model usually only focuses on the single alternative recommended for funding, not multiple alternatives.

BEST PRACTICES

66. DESIGN FIRST, SPREADSHEET LATER. A professional financial model is a piece of software and should be treated with the same rigor.

- Start with concepts. What decision does the model support and for whom?

- Next, calculations:

    - Separate "program" components, including calculations, of the model from data elements.

    - Use an input or assumptions sheet and ensure that assumptions are only entered once.

    - Lock calculation and data sections to stop inadvertent changes.

- Finally, calibrate, which means checking that the model forecasts realistically. When testing a model the purpose is to break the model, not to prove it works.

SEEK ASSURANCE THAT THE FINANCIAL MODEL IS ACCURATE

67. **STAY SIMPLE AND SMALL.** In the words of Michael Pidd, "model simple, think complicated" and "start small and add." Often a financial model is more complicated than the investment it aims to describe. In practice, the most difficult aspect of modeling is deciding which effects are important enough to include and which are not. A solid, usable model for an IT investment does not, typically, require spreadsheet wizardry and elaborate equations.

68. **APPLY THE TWO-MINUTE RULE: CAN YOU IDENTIFY THE KEY RESULTS OF SOMEONE'S MODEL WITHIN THE FIRST TWO MINUTES OF EXAMINING IT** (Stephen Powell, The Art of Modeling with Spreadsheets).

69. **EXTRACT AND EXAMINE THE KEY ASSUMPTIONS UNDERLYING ANY ROI MODEL:**

- What are the main assumptions in the model?

- Are the assumptions realistic? Are they expressed as a range of possible inputs?

- Is there a sensitivity analysis?

70. **SEEK ASSURANCE THAT THE FINANCIAL MODEL IS ACCURATE.**

- Raymond Panko's research into spreadsheet errors found per-cell or per-formula errors in 5.2% of the spreadsheets checked. Mercer Risk found 10% of project financing spreadsheets had errors.

- Who prepared it? Verify that a skilled person, who is independent of the project proposal team, has reviewed the financial model underlying the business case.

71. **ENSURE THAT THE TECHNOLOGY VENDOR VIEWS THE BUSINESS CASE AS A COMMITMENT, NOT A SELL-AND-FORGET ROI CALCULATOR.**

STEP TWELVE:
THE INVESTMENT DECISION

THE BUSINESS CASE SCORE PROVIDES A COMPACT SUMMARY OF THE OVERALL QUALITY OF A BUSINESS CASE AND ITS IT INVESTMENT. It allows collection and comparison of business case scores.

BEST PRACTICES

72. USE THE OVERALL BUSINESS CASE SCORE TO INFORM YOUR DECISION, NOT TO MAKE YOUR DECISION. The score is a rating of the quality of the business case and the underlying investment. A high score means that the business case is a good one and investing in it, combined with an active investment approach, is likely to deliver the forecasted returns. However, many factors come into play in delivering outcomes and results are never guaranteed. Good decisions can still have bad outcomes.

73. CAREFUL, CONSISTENT APPLICATION OF THIS CHECKLIST SHOULD PRODUCE BETTER IT INVESTMENT DECISIONS, BETTER INVESTMENT RESULTS, AND MORE SATISFIED SELLERS, BUYERS, AND USERS OF TECHNOLOGY.

SELECTED BIBLIOGRAPHY

Andriole, Stephen J. (2009). Technology Due Diligence: Best Practices for Chief Information Officers, Venture Capitalists, and Technology Vendors. Hershey, PA: Information Science Reference.

Agrell, Wilhelm, When Everything is Intelligence - Nothing is Intelligence, Sherman Kent Center for Intelligence Analysis.

Bierman, Harold, and Smidt, Seymour (2007). The Capital Budgeting Decision: Economic Analysis of Investment Projects. New York, New York: Routledge.

Bing, Gordon. (1996). Due Diligence Techniques and Analysis: Critical Questions for Business Decisions. Westport, Connecticut: Quorum Books.

Boehm, Barry W. and Sullivan Kevin J.; Software Economics: A Roadmap.

Booth, Wayne C., Colomb, Gregory G., and Williams, Joseph M. (2003).The Craft of Research. Chicago, Illinois: The University of Chicago Press.

Camp, Justin J. (2002). Venture Capital Due Diligence: A Guide to Making Smart Investment choices and Increasing Your Portfolio Returns. New York, New York: John Wiley & Sons, Inc.

CIA Directorate of Intelligence (1995). Compendium of Analytic Tradecraft Notes.

Devaraj, Sarv and Kohli, Rajiv (2002). The IT Payoff. Upper Saddle River, New Jersey: Prentice Hall PTR.

Dewar, James A. (2002). Assumption-Based Planning. Cambridge, United Kingdom: Cambridge University Press.

Gatiesh, Orit and MacArthur, Hugh (2008). Lessons from Private Equity Any Company Can Use. Boston, Massachusetts: Harvard Business School Press.

Gawande, Atul (2007). Better. A Surgeon's Notes on Performance. New York, New York: Picador.

IT Governance Institute, Enterprise Value: Governance of IT Investments, The Business Case.

Lanham, Richard (2000). Revising Business Prose. Needham Heights, Massuchusetts: Allyn & Bacon.

Levy, Frank and Murnane, Richard J. (2004). The New Division of Labor. Princeton, New Jersey: Princeton University Press.

Lovallo, Dan and Kahneman, Daniel. Delusions of Success: How Optimism Undermines Executives' Decisions. Harvard Business Review. (2003).

McConnell, Steve. (2006). Software Estimation. Redmond, Washington. Microsoft Press.

Pidd, Michael (1196). Tools for Thinking. New York, New York: John Wiley & Sons, Inc.

Powell, Stephen G. and Baker, Kenneth R. (2004). The Art of Modeling With Spreadsheets. New York, New York: John Wiley & Sons, Inc.

Razgaitis, Richard. (2003). Valuation and Pricing of Technology-Based Intellectual Property. Hoboken, New Jersey: John Wiley & Sons, Inc.

Scalia, Antonin and Garner, Bryan A. (2008). Making Your Case: The Art of Persuading Judges, St. Paul, Minnesota: Thomson/West.

Smith, Gerald F. (1998). Quality Problem Solving. Milwaukee, Wisconsin: ASQ Quality Press.

Smith, Janet K. and Smith, Richard L. (2000). Entrepreneurial Finance. New York, New York: John Wiley & Sons.

Spewak, Steven H. (1992). Enterprise Architecture Planning. New York, New York: John Wiley & Sons.

Steele, Robert David; The New Craft of Intelligence, OSS International Press, 2002.

Sugden, Robert and Williams, Alan (1978). The Principles of Practical Cost-Benefit Analysis. New York: Oxford University Press.

Thorp, John. (1998). The Information Paradox: Realizing the Business Benefits of Information Technology. McGraw-Hill.

Toulmin, Stephen E. (2003). The Uses of Argument. New York, New York: Cambridge University Press.

Treasury Board of Canada. An Enhanced Framework for the Management of Information Technology Projects (1998).

Ward, John, Daniel, Elizabeth, Peppard, Joe. Building Better Business Cases for IT Investments. MIS Quarterly Executive.

www.businesscasepro.com

NOTES

Made in the USA
San Bernardino, CA
24 February 2016